Own Job Action Learning

CREATING AND RUNNING YOUR OWN PROGRAMS

Copyright © George P Boulden

All Rights Reserved

No part of this book may be reproduced in any form,
by photocopying or by any electronic or mechanical means,
Including information storage or retrieval systems,
without permission in writing from both the copyright
owner and the publisher of this book.

ISBN 9781091624610

First Published November 2008

ALA INTERNATIONAL PUBLISHING

Lutterworth. England - alapub@ala-international.com

Email george.boulden@ala-international.com

Web site www.ala-international.com

Ed 6 March 2019

Contents

Synopsis 3
Acknowledgements 4
Action learning in Personal Development 5
    Traditional Own Job Programmes 6
    Bespoke Own Job Programmes 7
    Dual Focus programmes 8
    'Short' programmes 9
Creating Own Job Programmes 15
Example Case Studies 19
    Case 1 – Typical traditional Own Job proposal 19
    Case 2 – Combining Action Learning with Training 24
    Case 3 - Typical Own Job Programme 31
    Case 4 – Example of a Dual-focus programme 35
Further Reading 39

Synopsis

This is book two in our Action Learning series. Our goal in writing it is to provide those of you who are interested in the Own Job model with information that will help you create and run your own programmes.

Own job can be used to:

> - Develop people using 'own job' as the learning vehicle.
> - Re-inforce learning. For example where people have completed a skills development workshop, an action learning programme can be used to re-inforce the learning back in the workplace
> - Acquire new knowledge and skills. This would be relevant where a team is created to investigate a specific issue. Specialist support can be provided as part of the programme the learning from the experience can be captured through the addition of an action learning component. See Dual Focus programmes.

The book gives examples of these different applications of Own Job Action that we have worked with. It is based on our experience and shares our approach to the development of Own Job programmes. Other books in the series:

1. Applications of Action Learning
2. Own Job Action Learning
3. In-Plant Action Learning
4. Empowering Change through Facilitation

Acknowledgements

I would like to begin by acknowledging the great debt of gratitude I owe to Professor Reginald (Reg) Revans, the founder of the Action Learning movement. We met in 1974 when he was planning his first Action Learning programme in GEC. At the time of our first meeting I had recently transferred from line management into a management development role. I was very aware that mature managers did not respond well to 'teaching' and was searching for ways of creating learning opportunities. Over lunch Reg shared his ideas with me and I was sold; thirty-five years later I am still a convinced action learner. He introduced me to Alan Lawlor who pioneered Own Job Action Learning in the West Midlands and the three of us created Action Learning Associates (ALA) Intentional in 1980, to promote the application of Action Learning. My relationship with Reg continued until his death in 2003.

I would also like to acknowledge my good friends Malcolm Farnsworth and John Cooper. Malcolm as Principal of the Marconi Staff Development Centre in Chelmsford gave me the chance of a new career in management development which I have pursued for a very stimulating thirty-five years. John, who I worked with at Dunchurch Staff College, is a natural 'action learner' as anyone who has used or experienced the marvellous business simulations he created will testify and generous to a fault with everything he did. For me John is one of the unsung heroes of Action Learning and deserves to be recognised as such.

Finally I would like to acknowledge the many hundreds of participants and clients from around the globe who I have learned with and from over the years. It has been a great privilege to know you, thank you all.
George P Boulden, October 2014

Action learning in Personal Development

There are four main ways in which Action Learning can be used to develop individuals;

1. Unfamiliar / Unfamiliar – Participants undertake a different role, usually a project, in an unfamiliar environment.
2. Familiar / Unfamiliar – Participants undertake the same job in an unfamiliar environment. For example an accountant moves from a manufacturing to a retail environment.
3. Unfamiliar / Familiar – Participants undertake a different job in the same environment. The sales director transfers to the HR function.
4. Familiar / Familiar – Same job, same environment (Own Job).

The first three types programme all involve a considerable investment of both time and money and are therefore most appropriate for the development of high potential people; those who organizations see as their future leaders.

This book is concerned with our experience of 'Own Job' Programmes. These focus on the development of individuals within their own jobs. This is a simple, cost effective approach to developing people which delivers real results and avoids the expectation and re-entry problems often associated with job exchange and full time programmes. For more information on full time programmes please see the section on Further Reading to be found at the end of this book.

Own Job Programmes fall into two main groups'

Traditional - where the job is the focus for the identification and implementation of development needs and

Bespoke - where the model is adapted by the provider to meet specific needs.

Traditional Own Job Programmes

Reg ran his first 'action learning' programmes in the 1940's with Colliery Managers during his tenure as Director of Education with the National Coal Board in the United Kingdom. These were Own Job programmes where he encouraged Colliery managers to meet together in small groups, to share their experiences and ask each other questions about what they saw and heard. The approach led to significant increases in productivity and a reduction in accidents. These results reinforced his strongly held belief that conventional training in which University Professors stood up and talked about management could not deliver practical improvements in performance. Such improvements could only be achieved in his view by the people responsible for the work, working with others who are also committed to optimise performance and learning with and from each other.

Note. This concept 'working together' lies at the heart of the Japanese approach to productivity and was the driving force behind the Japanese productivity 'boom' in the 1970's.

The primary focus of 'traditional' Own Job Action Learning is personal development through the implementation of a work related project or it can be linked to some additional activity like bringing a new product to market, improving productivity, re-structuring the department et al.

Own job programmes are more informal than the other three types in that participants are often self-nominated; they are people who recognize the value of 'learning with and from each other'. As a result there is often no 'client' role in the formal sense; the participant's manager may only really be involved in giving permission and maybe authorizing funding. Thus, whilst these programmes use the classic five stage Action Learning model stage three and stage five reviews may not involve clients in the traditional sense.

The traditional model of Own Job is by far the most common application of Action Learning programmes and is alive and well today, at least in the UK. It appears to be most active in the Public Sector, Education, the Health Service, Local Authorities, The civil Service etc. These types of organisation seem to have become the 'natural' home of Own job programmes which would seem to indicate that people working in these environments relate well to the participative learning style which is the hallmark of Action Learning.

Bespoke Own Job Programmes

In addition to the traditional model there are 'special' programmes. These use the Own Job model but are 'tailored' by the provider to meet the specific client need. It seems to me that these can be divided into two groups

1. Dual focus programmes. These use Reg's five step structures but combine personal development with projects focused on specific performance goals. Such programmes vary in length depending on the complexity of the projects and usually involve two consultants an Action Learning and a specialist in the project area.
2. 'Short' programmes'. These use only one part of Reg's five stage model. For students for example the investigation phase can be a used for personal development when students are working on projects but there is no application as the programme ends with the presentation. In other cases, where we have people who have already identified their development needs the implementation phase of Own Job is perfect for providing the support necessary to empower them to achieve their development goals.

Dual Focus programmes

This first example is based on a development programme we ran in the Czech Republic for twelve companies. In addition to helping the management of these companies to re-structure their business we offered a number of 'bespoke own job' programmes where we streamed our participants by job category. We offered a Strategic Management programme for Managing Directors, a Managing with number programme for Finance Directors, a Best Practice programme for HR Directors, a Winning Business programme for Sales Directors etc. The sets were facilitated by specialists in the specific field by a facilitator. Meetings were held monthly on Saturdays during the life of the project. Participants were encouraged to share their experiences, to learn with and from each other and they were encouraged to adopt practices introduces by the specialists which they felt would be beneficial to their organisations. These meetings were very successful in both their personal and organisational development aims. This was especially true of the MD group. Eight of these were regular attendees and we organised visits to Japan for two of them to study 'best in class' businesses in their fields.

The second example explains how we used a 'dual focus' approach to deliver a combination of personal development and specialist training in performance improvement. My partner Alan Lawlor, who was a Qualified Method Study Engineer with thirty years' experience, turned the Own Job model into a 'Productivity Improvement' programme for small, mainly engineering business. He created a simple performance audit which participants completed monthly for their businesses and returned to him. He analysed the data and returned the results to set members prior to the monthly set meetings where it was used to help participants identify areas where they could 'learn with and from each other' about how to improve the productivity of their own businesses.

For a more detailed explanation of Alan's work see;

His book Productivity Improvement Manual – Alan Lawlor, Gower Press, ISBN0-566-02439-X

Note. Dual focus programmes like these differ from Traditional programmes in that there are two distinct roles,

1. The organisation and running of the programme and the facilitation of the learning.
2. The provision of relevant specialist advice,

Clearly if the specialist also has the interpersonal skills to facilitate the learning, as in Alan's case, the programme can be run by one consultant. However, as an example, we ran a very successful series of Productivity Improvement programmes for manufacturing companies in the Czech Republic. In this case I facilitated the learning and a consultant from Chu-San-Ren in Japan provided specialist advice on optimising productivity.

See Re-Engineering the Workplace – Available on our web site
http://www.amazon.co.uk/George-P.-Boulden/e/B001KHBJ34

'Short' programmes

Short programmes are another variant on the Own Job theme and use just part of the five step model. Some use the first phase of an Own Job programme as a vehicle for personal development whilst others, where development needs are known, they use the implementation phase to support participants behavioural change, AA, Weight Watchers, STOP smoking et al are good examples of this.

This, as I understand it, is now common practice in further education where Own Job programmes are used to encourage students to learn with and from each other. This captures the learning opportunities offered by the Investigation phase and can be used both to develop the students and to enable them to help each other with their projects. However as the outcome of the activity is a thesis which will only be used to evaluate the student's competence, there will be no implementation?

We have run a number of very successful programmes using just the Implementation phase. These are programmes where the development need or needs, which in a normal Action Leaning programme would be identified during the investigation phase, are already known. Thus the aim of the programme is to satisfy known development needs using the action learning methodology to support the learner through implementation. These programmes are shorter, usually three months rather than six and focused, we know what we are seeking to do from the start. We have used two approaches to this type of programme;

1. Adding an Implementation phase to a modular training programme. At the end of each module participants were encouraged to identify learning needs they had identified during the training. Sets were created and a series of meeting to review progress which each participant would report on at the beginning of the next module.

2. Identify learning needs through auditing existing development programmes which can then be satisfied using the implementation phase of an Own Job Action Learning programme.

Using the Implementation phase to support behavioural change

The following example is taken from a programme we ran for a large Local Government organisation in the UK. The remit was to create a Leadership programme that would help to turn middle managers into leaders. This envisaged an eight stage modular programme running over four months.

1. Introduction by senior management – ½ day
2. Managers as Leaders – 2 days
3. Personal development project based on the learning from module 2 – 1 month

4. Review of the learning and module on Team Working - 1 day
5. Personal development project based on the learning from module 4 – 1 month
6. Review of the learning and module on Coaching - 1 day
7. Personal development project based on the learning from module 6 – 1 month
8. Final review of the programme carried out in-house by the Training Manager sponsors.

We ran five of these programmes over two years. Of the 92 potential participants who attended the Introductory meeting 76 volunteered to attend the workshops; of these 30% were seen by their managers to have achieved significant changes in job performance 50% showed some improvement and only 20% showed little or no improvement. Whilst the Action Learning part of the programme was 'informal' in that we did not plan meetings during the implementation process, for those who wanted to do something, it worked well. There was ample evidence of informal meetings and people working together supporting Reg's contention that just a little encouragement, we can and do 'learn with and from each other'

Why was it so successful? I believe it was because;

1. The proposed actions were discussed in plenary and those with common ground were encouraged to work together
2. All were encouraged to meet at least once before the next module in one month's time
3. They were also given a contact in HR where they could seek help.
4. The 'projects' were recorded and sent to participants within a couple of days of the end of the workshop.
5. They knew we would ask them what they had achieved at the start of the next module; fear of looking foolish in front of one's colleagues is a great motivator.

These factors helped to create sufficient motivation to ensure that most participants did something. I am not suggesting this approach as an alternative to traditional Action Learning, what I am proposing is that using the gaps between training modules to focus on personal development and encouraging participants to work on needs identified during the 'training' modules is much more efficient that training alone. See Case 2 in the following chapter for more detailed information.

Note. In my view enormous amounts of time and money are wasted on behavioural training not because there is anything wrong with the training but because it is not possible in short training programmes to achieve the behavioural change necessary to enable most participants to become skilled interviewers, charismatic leaders, win / win negotiators et al. Human behaviour is determined by individual values and environment. Thus for me to become a more effective leader, I must take my training back into the workplace and practice using it to develop my leadership skills until they become a habit.

Most large organisations, at one time or another, run what we 'sheep dip' programmes. Someone decides that all first line managers will attend a, for example, Communication Skills workshop and they do. So what? How many organisations firstly realise that the behavioural change necessary to change poor communicators into good communicators cannot, in most cases be achieved in a three day workshop; you can only begin the process. Secondly how many organisations assess the results of such programmes? Not many I guess. The following is an example from a company which carried out effectiveness assessment, what they found and what they did about it.

In 2000 Roche Pharma introduced, with London Business School, 'Insights for Pharma' a four-day 360-development program designed to develop Pharma senior manager's leadership skills. One of the divisions which supported the program, Pharma Development (PD), identified from research carried out in early 2002 that, whilst the majority of their participants found the workshops personally satisfying, many reported finding it difficult applying their learning in the workplace. PD management decided to introduce a voluntary Own Job Action Learning, called Peer Group Learning (PGL) to provide local support for those Insights participants wishing to develop their leadership competencies in their working environment

The programme was introduced at PD's three main sites in the US, UK and Switzerland in November 2002 with 49 of the 95 Insights alumni deciding to participate. These were formed into nine sets facilitated by the local HR community who were trained and supported by external specialist in each country. A review was conducted in May 2003 after all sets had met six times. This found that participants both enjoyed the experience and felt it had helped them to achieve their development goals with more than 50% having begun a second phase of development. They valued the discipline imposed by the set meetings, the facilitation, the opportunity to share experiences and to learn with and from each other. 86% reported the overall value of the PGL process as good or excellent. Based on these findings management decided that PGL should continue as an integral part of Insights.

PGL was offered to all Insights participants until the Insights program ended in November 2004. A final review in early 2005 found that a further hundred people had participated in PGL sets and that the process was alive and well. Six sets were operational in the US, eight in Switzerland, two of which were 'virtual' and four sets in the UK. There was also clear evidence of secondary activity on all three sites with participants using the process in their own work areas indicating that the learning style suits the Roche culture of individual empowerment. Participants again reported they enjoyed the experience and it had helped them to achieve their development goals.

See Case 3 in the following chapter for more information.

Note. In my view Action learning programmes without implementation are like eating food without salt. Investigation is interesting but implementation, getting things done in practice, is the real test. The investigation phase is like the courtship before a marriage, implementation is more like the marriage itself.

Creating Own Job Programmes

I believe that the key to success in any enterprise is the market. If there is no market for your product there is no money for you. In Action Learning we have a product which improves effectiveness and therefore productivity but how do you sell it? It's based on participation and empowering the people and sadly, in my experience traditional managers are not very keen on that. You can look for clients who believe in empowerment. You can also look for Dual Focus and Short Programme opportunities. So the first question is;

Who are your potential customers?

What problems do they have that your product can solve?

What type of Own Job programme would be relevant to them?

Who are the decision makers?

Why you? What is your USP? Your Unique Selling Point, what makes you different?

Once you have an idea of your product there are two main routes to market for anyone who would like to offer Action Learning programmes. These are open programmes and bespoke programmes.

Open programmes are usually offered directly to the participant. They are pre-planned and you know what you are getting before you start. They are most appropriate for organisations that have a client base like Universities, Business Schools, Trade Associations that offer training to members or Professional Associations like The Chartered Institute of Personnel and Training in the UK etc. They can also work where you have no client base but have a USP in your offering like Alan Lawlor with his Productivity Audit Programmes for Small Business which was supported by the Institute of Works Management.

Bespoke programmes on the other hand are 'pulled' by the market. You as a supplier are invited to tender for a programme. When we created ALA International we decide that this was the market for us for two reasons. Firstly, with Reg as a Partner we had enormous credibility. I had been working for four years at this time with Action Learning at Dunchurch College of Management and Alan was well known for his work in the West Midlands. Secondly, Open programmes unless you are working in a known market are a 'hard' sell and nowhere near as interesting for us as designing programmes to satisfy specific needs.

To start the process you need invitations to tender. How do you get them? In the usual way, through people you know and by building your network. Writing up your successes, going to places where potential clients go, seeking chances talk about Action Learning and so on.

You receive your first invitation, what now? You need to gather information from the client and use that information to create a winning proposal. Normally you will have some information from the client in the request for tender but this will not be enough to create a successful proposal.

Our approach is to start with the structure of the proposal. If it is an official tender you will be given the format in which the client would like to receive the information. However, in most cases in our experience, we decide the format of the proposal and have found the following structure works well:

Action Learning Programme

Prepared by: George Boulden, ALA International Ltd

Prepared for:

Date: 9 April 2019

Contents:

Introduction
Objectives
For
Method
Programme
Expected Outcomes
Budget

We use the structure of the proposal as a check list. Start by filling in what we know. For example we know who the client is and we know the method – Action Learning but we often don't know much else. So make a list and ask the client, if possible face to face. Why face to face?

1. Because it's an opportunity to start to build rapport
2. You can see as well as hear so it's much easier to pick up on the nuances it's so easy to miss on the telephone

3. You can reflect in the proposal the actual words the client used

The following is an example of a check list we used to tender for a recent contract:

Meeting 26th XYZ Company

- Introduce yourself
- Ask about the Company
- Objectives for the programme
- Who is the programme for
- Method – share how you see the programme
- Expected Outcomes – what results are they looking for from the programme
- Budget – Is there a budget? What do they expect to pay?
- Thank you – What happens next? I will …

With this information we can then produce a proposal see example cases in the next chapter.

Example Case Studies

Case 1 – Typical traditional Own Job proposal

Action Learning Programme for XYZ Industries

Prepared by: George Boulden, ALA International Ltd

Prepared for: Alan Smith, HR Director, XYZ Industries

Date: 9 April 2019

Contents:

Introduction
Objectives
For
Method
Programme
Expected Outcomes
Budget

Own Job Action Learning Programme for XYZ Industries

INTRODUCTION

This proposal results from recent meeting with Alan Smith, HR Director of XYZ Industries to discuss his request for a proposal for an Own Job Action Learning programme. The proposal envisages a traditional Own Job programme (see Annex A of this proposal for more information) that will run in six stages starting with a briefing session for sponsoring managers and participants. The briefing (i) will cover the nature of the Action Learning philosophy and (ii) show participants how to identify a job related problem for the learning project. Stage two will be a three day launch workshop during which delegates receive training in problem solving and group working skills and carry out the initial work on their project. Stage three involves the delegates investigating their problems and proposing recommendations. In stage four the recommendations are presented to sponsoring managers and implementation plans agreed. In stage five the participants implement these. Stage six is a review during which the success of the programme is assessed and the learning agreed.

OBJECTIVES

1. To solve real business problems
2. To develop participants interpersonal skills
3. To create the capability for ongoing learning

FOR

Supervisors and managers from XYZ Industries

METHOD

The programme uses the 'Action Learning' approach. This is based on three guiding principles:

1. People learn best from reflected practice, by stepping back and thinking about what they are doing and why.
2. The best test of any learning is to try it out in action.
3. The learning process is greatly strengthened by regularly sharing the experience with those who are also learning by doing.

PROGRAMME

Stage 1 – *'Setting the stage'* ½ day

A 'briefing note' is issued to all participants and sponsoring managers. ALA will conduct a briefing workshop on the philosophy behind the programme for participants and their managers. As part of this briefing managers and participants are asked to agree the learning projects before the Launch Workshop. Note a Performa setting out the format for writing up the project will be provided and all projects will be reviewed by the consultants before the Launch Workshop.

Stage 2 - *Launch Workshop [3 days]*

This three-day workshop is designed to create the *Action Learning Set*. During the first two days participants will be introduced to the basic problem solving, team working and communication skills they will need to work with during the programme. The third day will be spent working as a set on individual projects. The Set has the following features:

1. Between 5-7 members who meet once every two to three weeks.

2. A coordinator. This role is taken by all set members in rotation. The coordinator organises and chairs the meeting and writes up the minutes. Note. These are a simple record of what each participant agrees to do before the next meeting and will be used as its agenda.
3. A facilitator who helps the group to work effectively together as they assist one another to achieve the goals of their projects. He/she also captures the individual learning and personal growth and development that is taking place. (Normally the consultant acts as the facilitator but internal personnel with the appropriate skills can take this role.)

Stage 3 - *Investigation and Recommendation stage [3 months]*

Set members investigate the issues facing them in their projects, look at alternatives and propose a course of action. Set meetings are held once every two to three weeks with the facilitator in attendance.

Stage 4 - *Presentation and Feedback [1/2 day]*

This is a plenary meeting with all participants and their clients. Participants present their findings and recommendations in the plenary; the clients are asked to decide which of the recommendations should be implemented.

Stage 5 – *Implementation [3 months]*

The participants work to implement the actions agreed with their clients. The set and the adviser continue to meet once every two weeks.

Stage 6 – *Review [1/2 day]*

Set members and clients meet to assess what has/has not been achieved and agree the way ahead.

BUDGET

Stage 1 - Preparation and Briefing - 3 days
Stage 2 - Introductory workshop - 3 days
Stage 3 - 6 x 1 day consultancy visits
Stage 4 - Attending 1 day review session
Stage 5 - 6 x 1 day consultancy visits
Stage 6 - Attending 1 day review session

Note. This budget assumes that there will be 2 sets

[All plus travel, accommodation, training materials, manuals, & VAT]

Case 2 – Combining Action Learning with Training

In chapter 2 we quoted the example of a Leadership Master Class programmes that we ran for a Regional Authority in the UK. In this case the programme was designed working with the head of training. There were a number of iteration before we reached what became the final version which was presented by us to the senior team, see copy below.

"Becoming Competent Leaders"
Leadership Skills Development Programme

XXX County Council

Setting the Scene – (Module 1)

There is compelling evidence to demonstrate that adults learn most effectively from training and development when they can see a reason for doing it, are stimulated by it and can relate the development activity to the 'bigger picture'. This introductory module is designed to present each of these three elements to the delegates.

In addition, this module will provide a point of reference for the other modules in the programme, enabling delegates to place the activities in context.

The format for this module will be a presentation by the senior managers from the Environment Directorate, who will introduce the Leadership Programme in terms of:

- Vision and goals of the directorate
- Challenges of Best Value
- The need to develop leaders as opposed to managers
- Feedback from the staff survey and the EFQM self-assessment
- The Leadership Development programme in context with other development initiatives
- The links to the management competencies

The module will conclude with an introduction to The PROSPER Group and a short question and answer session.

Whilst the programme will be delivered by the directorate management, BSK will provide advice on content and format, if required.

Managers as Leaders – (Module 2)

High performing teams need high performing leadership. This module is designed to develop the essential skills of leaders and considers what is involved in motivating a team

For:

Managers/team leaders and anyone involved in leading work, projects or teams.

Objectives:

To clarify the role of the leader
To understand the 'process' of team leadership
To explore leadership styles
To identify and practice leadership skills

Content:

- The role of leader – What do leaders do? What is the difference between managers and leaders?
- Leadership theory and styles – Situational leadership, Action centred leadership, Management by walking around (MBWA)
- Motivational theories - McGregor, Herzberg and Maslow
- Self-assessment of personal style - Diagnostic questionnaire
- The beliefs of successful leaders – Attitude, self-belief, self-efficacy, effective mind sets
- The expectations of followers – Review of research into the expectations of followers; Five key behaviours: Modelling the way, Enabling, Inspiring, Challenging, Forward looking.
- Empowerment – What is empowerment? How to? Pitfalls to avoid
- Cultural values and style – The impact of organisational culture and personal style on motivation
- Commitment & rewards – Personal recognition vs financial reward
- Target setting & delegation – Performance management processes; links to situational leadership and personal style

- Communication and information flow – Methodologies
- Monitoring & controlling progress – Performance management; coaching; feedback

TWO DAY PROGRAMME (plus 'Action Learning' projects to be reviewed in module three)

Leading Effective Teams – (Module 4)

In order to achieve in today's competitive market place, organisations are realising that by creating effective teams they can ensure that a strategy, which focuses on the organisational goals, is implemented and achieved. This programme is designed to enable your managers to lead and develop teams, to build their people into a 'high performance' unit and to lead teams through a process of change.

For:

All managers who lead or facilitate teams.

Objectives:

1. To develop participants understanding of the nature of team working and empowerment
2. To clarify the roles of team leader & team coach
3. To enhance participants skills through the use of practical exercises
4. To explore the role of the leader in a change process

Content:

- Purpose & value of team working – Why teams? Benefits of teamwork
- Vision & values – Developing team vision and shared values

- Team work Vs group work – Exploring the differences in approach and output;
- Beliefs of 'expert' team leaders & coaches – Attitude; Expectations; Self Efficacy
- Understanding the 'needs' of the team – Links to situational leadership; team dynamics
- Skills development – Skills of the team leader; Facilitation; Developing the skills of the team
- Developing openness & trust – In the leader and within the team
- Setting specific goals for the team – Performance management techniques; Performance measures
- Role of each individual in the team – Identifying preferred team roles; Refreshing Belbin; Building on team strengths
- Feedback on performance – Giving effective feedback; Positive reinforcement; Improving performance
- Attitudes towards change – How people react to change; Creating a positive frame for change; The effect of change on team performance
- The role of the leader in a change process – a strategy for leading a high performing team through change

ONE DAY PROGRAMME (plus 'Action Learning' projects to be reviewed in module 5)

The Leader as Coach – (Module 6)

This programme aims to provide managers with the skills of coaching so that the support they give their team is effective and well received. The programme runs in two stages starting with a one-day skills workshop which will focus on developing a quick, *informal* style of coaching. In stage two the delegates try out their skills in practice by implementing coaching projects on their return to work. During this stage the 'coaches' meet in an Action Learning Set to share their experiences and learn with and from each other.

For:

Managers and team leaders who coach others as part of their work.

Objectives:

1. To provide an understanding of the role of the coach
2. To develop coaching and counselling skills
3. To improve the performance of both managers/team leaders and thus the performance of their teams.

Content:

- Development options – exploration of a range of coaching approaches, to suit individual needs and varying situations
- Identifying the need – Links to performance management; The purpose of coaching
- Beliefs of 'expert' coach's - Attitudes; Expectations; Self Efficacy
- Setting coaching tasks – Frameworks; Objectives; checking understanding
- Coaching skills – Questioning; Facilitation; Feedback
- Values & style – Personal beliefs; Links to situational leadership
- Coaching cross functional teams

ONE DAY PROGRAMME (plus 'Action Learning 'sets for ongoing development)

Workplace application – (Modules 3 and 5)

During these modules delegates will apply the knowledge and skills gained during the previous module, to the working environment. Delegates will be encouraged to network with their colleagues, thus building not only on their own experience, but also on the experience of others.

These stages will ensure the following outcomes are achieved:

1. Knowledge and skill is applied and developed
2. Delegates receive feedback from their peers and teams

Case 3 - Typical Own Job Programme

This proposal was for the development of Business Advisors. It was designed to satisfy the organisation's need to meet the CPD (Continuing Professional Development) requirements for professional people to undertake a minimum of three days off job training annually. It differs from from traditional Own Job programmes in that it starts with a two day workshop.

BUSINESS ADVISER DEVELOPMENT PROGRAMME – 4 MONTHS

Introduction

This Development Centre is designed to provide a development opportunity for Business Advisers. It is uses a competency-based approach based on the SFEDI Common Core Standards. It combines assessment with Continuing Professional Development and runs in three main stages starting with a two-day workshop followed by a three month Action Learning programme to support the CPD.

Objectives

The objectives of this programme are yo:-

1. Provide a development opportunity for BA's
2. Ensure the professional competence of BA's
3. Directly impact the profitability of the client organisation

Programme

The programme runs in three stages over four months as follows:

Stage 1 – Development Centre – 2 days – 11th and 12th November

This provides participants with the opportunity to assess themselves against the SFEDI Common Core Standards. They will receive 360-degree assessment from colleagues and clients together with advice and personal mentoring to help them create an appropriate CPD programme, see detailed programme attached.

Stage 2 – Action Learning Phase - 3 months – December / February

Participants will be formed into Action Learning sets which will meet for half a day every three weeks with a facilitator to review their projects and to learn with and from each other about the process of learning. It is proposed that there will be five meetings during this period culminating in the one-day review.

Stage 3 - Review - 1 day – 16th March 2004

The day will provide an opportunity to review what has/has not been achieved during the programme and to agree on the next steps. As part of this process participants will be asked to carry out a further 360 degree assessment involving both colleagues and clients to evaluate their development.

BUSINESS ADVISER
DEVELOPMENT CENTRE WORKSHOP 10/11th NOVEMBER

Introduction

This workshop is designed to provide participants with an opportunity to review their development needs using the SFEDI Common Core Standards. The programme runs in three stages beginning with an introductory workshop focusing on self-assessment using 360-degree feedback from colleagues and clients, structured activities and mentoring. It enables participants to objectively assess their development needs and to create practical development plans, which can be actioned in the next stage of the programme.

Objectives

1. To provide BA's with the opportunity to objectively review their development needs in the current job using the SFEDI Common Core Standards as the base line.
2. To help participants to create realistic development projects for achieving them.
3. To provide ongoing support during the development phase to ensure that development needs are met.

For

Current and potential Business Advisers in Business Link and the wider Business support network

Method

The workshop will use a combination of self and peer assessment to create a current performance profile and help individuals to create appropriate personal development plans.

Syllabus

The workshop is based on the SFEDI Common Core Standards.

Outline programme

Stage 1 – Development Centre Workshop 2 days

Note – Performance assessments will be collected from participants, the sponsoring manager, peers and selected clients prior to the workshop and used as part of the feedback.

Day 1

0900 – 0915	Introduction & Objectives
0915 – 0945	Personal introductions
0945 – 1030	Successful Personal Development
1100 – 1230	The Business Adviser role – Exercise
1330 - 1545	Structured interviews
1545 – 1700	Winning the Business (Getting to Yes)– Role Play
1700 – 1800	Diagnosing Performance Problems – Exercise
2000	External Speaker

Day 2:

0830 – 0900	Story Board
0900 – 1030	Value Relating Styles / Emotional Intelligence – Feedback and mentoring
1100 – 1230	Identifying value adding opportunities - Exercise
1330 -- 1400	Introduction to CPD
1400 – 1415	Competencies report and Personal Development Planning
1415 – 1600	Individual feedback and mentoring - producing Personal Development Plan
1600 – 1700	Creating Continuous Development Sets, first meeting
1700	Review and Close

Case 4 – Example of a Dual-focus programme

This example, referred to earlier shows how we organised a dual focus consultancy programme in practice.

JAPANESE METHODS PROGRAMME PRODUCTIVITY IN PRACTICE

This programme is run jointly by ALA International Ltd, and Chu-San-Ren of Japan. The programme has three main aims:-

1. To enable companies to improve productivity through using appropriate Japanese Management Methods to solve a specific problem
2. To create a cadre of people in participating companies who can continue the work started in the programme
3. The provide a development opportunity for the people who participate in the programme

In preparation for the workshops companies are asked to select a specific process they would like to improve and to nominate a cross-functional team of seven people to be responsible for improving it. Each company is visited prior to the start of the programme to assess the proposed projects for viability and to write Terms of Reference. All teams were given a pre workshop briefing and copies of the workshop materials, which they were asked to read before the start of the programme. The programme, which lasts eleven days, starts with a three-day intensive workshop. This is divided into two parts, the morning sessions are devoted to providing a detailed explanation of JIT and KAIZEN. The afternoon session focus on training in team working skills, with the third afternoon being used to prepare the teams for their in-company projects. The teams then have three days back in the host companies to investigate the problem and decide what to do with the consultants visiting each team for half a day on site during this period. The teams then spend a further day in plenary where they present their findings and proposed actions and are helped to prepare for the management presentation the following day. The teams spend the next three days back in the company. They make a presentation to management setting out their findings and recommendations, agree the action plans and start the implementation process, again with consultancy support. The final day of the programme is spent carrying out a plenary review to assess the results, participants personal learning and the next steps in the process. See annex A for detailed programme. Teams are expected to demonstrate some measurable achievement within the life of the programme and have a plan in place to complete the project within an agreed time scale.

ANNEX A

JAPANESE METHODS PROGRAMME
PRODUCTIVITY IN PRACTICE

Day 1 0800 - 0900 Introduction and Objectives
        0900 - 1200 The Japanese Approach to Productivity
                            Problems of Quality and Productivity
                            JIT and KANBAN
        1230 - 1600 Introduction to Team Working
                            The Action Learning Approach
                            Team working tools
                            Meetings
                            Logical Problem Solving,
                            Presenting with Impact
                            Interpersonal Communication
                            Being Assertive
                            SWOT, Process Mapping,
                            Fish Bone,
                            Creative Thinking

Day 2 0800 - 1200 Introduction to Kaizen
                            Philosophy
                            The tools
                            Start with measurement
                            Quality, time, costs,
                            Waste weeding and other tools
        1230 - 1600 Team working tools continued

Day 3 0800 - 1200 Starting the project - initial appraisal
                            Agreeing the terms of reference
        1230 - 1600 Preparing the action plan

Day 4/6	Working on company projects. Note The consultants visit each project team in the host company during this period

Day 7 0830 - 1030 -Review and prepare presentations
        1100 - 1230 Presentations and feedback
        1330 - 1500 Plan for in-company presentations
        1530 - 1730 Preparation and final rehearsal

Days 8/10	Teams present their findings to senior management in host Companies Agree action plan Carryout initial implementation Note. The consultants visit each project team in the host company during this period
Day 11	Plenary review. Teams report on what they have / have not achieved Review the learning points and the way ahead

Further Reading

If you have found reading this book interesting you may you may also find the following useful.

1. To learn more about 'action learning' I recommend Reg's original book on the subject 'The ABC of Action Learning' Published by Gower Publications, ISBN 978-1-4094-2703-2

2. If you would like to learn more about Facilitation then 'Facilitating Action Learning: A Practitioner's Guide' by <u>Mike Pedler</u> and <u>Christine Abbott</u> is a useful read. Also David Casey's excellent paper on The Emerging Role of the Set Advisers, copies available from ALA International

3. For more about the Unfamiliar job Familiar environment model used in the GEC Action Learning programmes see; More Than Management Development, Ed Davis Casey & Davis Pearce, Gower, 1977 ISBN 0 566 02005 X

4. For more about the Unfamiliar job – Unfamiliar Environment model used in the Belgium Exchange programme see; Developing Effective Managers, Reginald W Revans Praeger,1971, Library of Congress 70-95689.

Books George has written on Action Learning and related topics

The following books are published by ALA International. They are available on our web site www.ala-international.com and from **Google Books** and **Amazon** in Epub, PDF and paperback formats.

Books about Action learning

Applications of Action Learning – describes the philosophy of action learning and its applications. ISBN 978-0-9560822-4-4

Own Job Action Learning – describes how Action learning can be used in individual development programmes. ISBN 978-0-9560822-0-6

In-Plant Action Learning – explains how the philosophy of Action learning can be used to deliver organisational change. ISBN 978-0-9560822-3-7

In-Plant Action Learning Teams, Participants Guide – This Guide is designed to help In-Plant teams to self-manage and facilitate their own learning; available from ALA International.

Empowering Change through Facilitation – describes how the process of facilitation is used to develop participants in Action Learning sets. ISBN 978-0 -9560822-9-9

Books about Personal Development

Managers as Leaders - This book show how management and leadership combine to ensure the effective delivery of the task. ISBN 978-0-9560822-2-0

Managing Difficult Relationships – examines the reasons for difficult relationships and provides a 'framework' for negotiating win / win solutions. ISBN 978-0-9560822-5-1

Change; Become a Winner - I believe that life is not a rehearsal, it's a journey and you can change it. If you would like to do something different with your life this book is for you. ISBN 13 978-1503185401, ISBN 10:1503185400

Books about Productivity

Productivity Improvement Manual – Alan Lawlor, Gower Press, ISBN0-566-02439-X

Values & Style; the Key to Productivity –The common denominator in performance improvement in organizations, is managing style. The things that stop people doing the best job they can stem from 'them and us' attitudes. These are based on cultural values and determine the way human beings perceive their roles and relationships within hierarchies. This book explores the nature of values and style and how they impact the operating effectiveness of organizations and societies.

Re-Engineering the Workplace – This book describes the Japanese approach to productivity with practical examples on how it can be applied in practice.

Useful web sites for Action Learning

Action Learning is a worldwide network. The following are some useful contacts in the Action Learning world:-

The International Foundation for Action Learning (IFAL), formally The Action Learning Trust www.ifal.org.uk

International Community of Action Learners (ICAL) This is a loose federation of Action Learning practitioners. Their web site can be found on www.tlainc.com

IMC acts as a clearing house for academic institutions offering Action Learning programmes. Contact www.imc.org.uk/imcal-inter
For articles www.free-press.com/journals/gaja

The Revans Library at Salford University www.salford.ac.uk

World Institute for Action Learning, www.wial.com

Please use the following link to find our books on Amazon.

http://www.amazon.com/s?ie=UTF8&page=1&rh=n%3A283155%2Cp_27%3AGeorge%20Boulden

I will be very grateful if you will take a few minutes to write a review on this book while you are there. Thank you.

George Boulden

www.ingramcontent.com/pod-product-compliance
Lightning Source LLC
Chambersburg PA
CBHW030737180526
45157CB00008BA/3208